Toni Maisey is a volunteer in Emergency at Princess Margaret Hospital which is now Perth Children's Hospital, and volunteers in a museum as a designer.

Toni is a mother of five children, a nurse assistant, graphic designer, artist, illustrator, student and an ex-owner of a Christian gallery/café.

Toni is a Roman Catholic/Christian healer and prays in the name of Jesus but enjoys healing all from different religions and those that don't believe in anything spiritual.

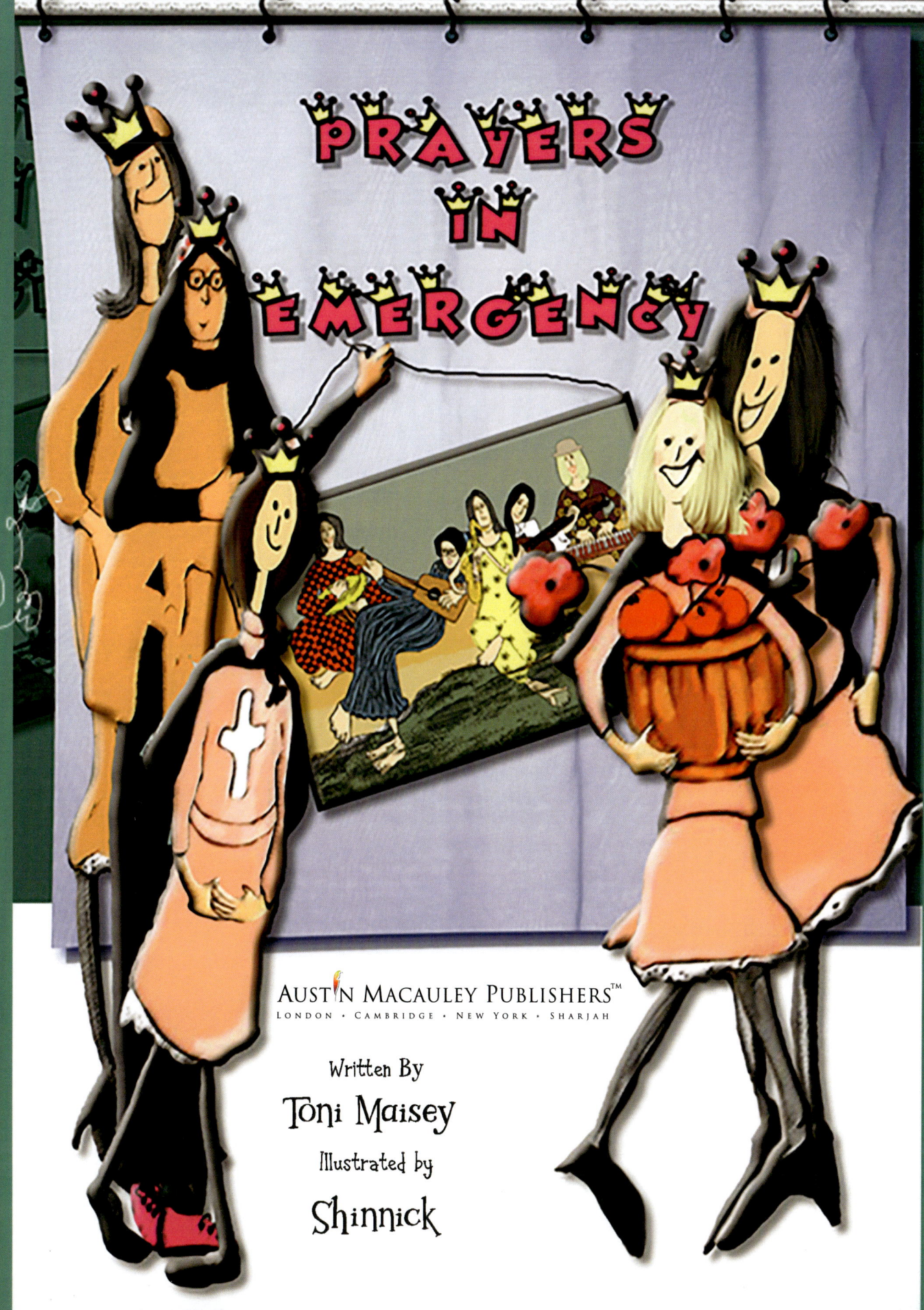

PRAYERS IN EMERGENCY

Austin Macauley Publishers™
LONDON • CAMBRIDGE • NEW YORK • SHARJAH

Written By
Toni Maisey

Illustrated by
Shinnick

Copyright © Toni Maisey (2020)
Illustrated by Shinnick

The right of **Toni Maisey** and **Shinnick** to be identified as author and illustrator of this work has been asserted by them in accordance with section 77 and 78 of the Copyright, Designs and Patents Act 1988.

All rights reserved. No part of this publication may be reproduced, stored in a retrieval system, or transmitted in any form or by any means, electronic, mechanical, photocopying, recording, or otherwise, without the prior permission of the publishers.

Any person who commits any unauthorised act in relation to this publication may be liable to criminal prosecution and civil claims for damages.

A CIP catalogue record for this title is available from the British Library.

ISBN 9781528909204 (Paperback)
ISBN 9781528959193 (ePub e-book)

www.austinmacauley.com

First Published (2020)
Austin Macauley Publishers Ltd
25 Canada Square
Canary Wharf
London
E14 5LQ

This book is dedicated to Princess Margaret Hospital Emergency staff who over the years helped me to see what real heroes and legends look like.

Dear Emergency at Princess Margaret Hospital,

I would like to thank all of Emergency for inspiring me to write this book; Emergency has been my motivation for continuing to improve my knowledge and wisdom of how wonderful God and medical work together.

I also thank my beautiful children: Robert, Jodi, Therese, Jack and Rory and my beautiful grandchildren; Tahlia, Sascha, Elijah and Ari and my future grandchildren.

I'd really like to thank Emergency again for they are all the characters in the book and how they provided me with the opportunity create this story for sick children who need to know that they are going to get well again.

And a big thanks to the Mandurah Community Museum whose creative employees and volunteers helped me to bring this book together.

The children's book tells the true events of miracles (names removed) happening in a main children's hospital in Perth where the parents, doctors and nurses and secretaries allowed me to pray when children were too sick in emergency.

In Emergency, I volunteered and helped the nurses and the parents and the children by calming them down with stories and toys. I started to see too many sick children and as a healer, I started praying. When God's anointing was strong, I would pray for the child that needed it most.

The most beautiful thing about praying in emergency is that religions come together in agreement for prayer, all nationalities of different religions Muslims, Catholics and even Atheists allow the healing, as they all put away their prejudice and focus on the children's recovery.

I believe God removes cancer faster than medicine, but I believe that God and medical science work together to save the children. And when a real emergency happens and a child might die, God can reverse that whereas medicine cannot.
Where there is brain damage from an accident and God is there, he can completely heal them. Meningitis is another one illness where God's prayers will stop it taking a life. I have seen many miracles that God has done and this book explains a few in a funny way. It is a story taken from true events made with fictional characters. However, if you ever walk into emergency on a Saturday morning, you would see the book come alive because all the characters are there.

This book is to give hope to children, who are suffering in hospitals, that with a great God, healing is possible and will not fail them. God can send in great healers who are not religious but when the healers belong to God they will not fail to heal. But like all things, too much medicine, food or drinks can hurt the body so, Jesus heals but he also says go and sin no more.

John 5:14
Afterward Jesus findeth him in the temple, and said unto him, Behold, thou art made whole: sin no more, lest a worse thing come unto thee.

6

CONTENTS

PRAYING IN EMERGENCY by TONI MAISEY.

1 Timothy 4:4–5
For everything created by God is good, and nothing is to be rejected if it is received with thanksgiving, for it is made holy by the word of God and prayer.

'The outpouring of the Holy Spirit in a Hospital where Heaven's door opens in Emergency'

'BLESSING THE HANDKERCHIEFS'

"Aaaaahhhhh," cried the nurse. "Its pigs."

I think when I heard this, I knew it was flu season again, swine flu, no, just flues, coughs and bronchitis. My name is Toni and I have been volunteering in emergency once or twice a week, seeing many wonderful healings through God and medical working together. The nurses, doctors and secretaries are always stressed just in case they might lose a child and when you know God doesn't fail to heal everyone in the room, it takes fear of all.

As a Roman Catholic Christian healer, I love to pray for those that are very ill and always ask in prayer who the anointing is mainly for. There are always many families from diverse cultures but they are always welcoming and ask for prayer from me.

I also love to bless all the teddy bears and puppets that the lady volunteers knit together.

(In the old days, they would bless the handkerchiefs and give them as gifts to the sick and send them to the men and women in the wars).

Psalm 41:3
The LORD sustains them on their sickbed
and restores them from their bed of illness.

'CAR ACCIDENT'

On this particular morning in emergency, all the nurses were running around busy, when suddenly St John's Ambulance paramedics rushed in bringing in a little Asian two-year- old girl and her four-year-old brother that had been in a car accident.

I felt the Lord's presence arrive in emergency as the situation looked critical. The power of God was strong, I knew God was there. I could see the holiness of the Lord surround the emergency. The doctors and nurses worked quickly and went into action as the little girl was white and very still. The girl woke up crying as her parents had not arrived yet and the nurses and doctors had to calm her down as they prepared the oxygen and all the equipment they might need, in case she got worse. The boy was stable, and the parents arrived, still quite dazed but were there to make sure their children were okay. I was worried and had been standing near the little girl and looking after the boy to calm him down. I didn't leave until I knew God had healed her and her brother. I prayed later for their healing with the blessing of the parents. Jesus was there, God does not fail ever.

John 14:13

Whatever you ask in my name, this I will do, that
the Father may be glorified in the Son.

'SMALL PRAYERS ARE POWERFUL'

Late in the afternoon, the hospital felt like a church as God's presence became stronger and I saw God's
angels arriving to help us in emergency as there were many sick children.

I sometimes cry in the kitchen because I don't like to think that children experience a lot of pain.

The angels showed me they were helping the nurses to relax more and letting them know that God was
doing the healing today (which may seem a funny thing to say to a doctor or nurse, but God is more
powerful and that's a fact).

Later, St John's Ambulance paramedics brought in a little girl who was involved in a car accident and
wasn't moving and was in shock.

I went over to her parents to offer refreshments and to say hello. They asked me to say a prayer for their
daughter as they were frightened that she would not get better.

After the prayer, the girl became more alert and delighted them when she jumped up out of bed
bouncing and running around smiling. God is so great; his miracles are amazing.

(God also heals without you feeling his power because feelings might not be from God).

Matthew 11:28–30

Come to me, all who labour and are heavy laden, and I will give you rest. Take my yoke upon you, and learn from me, for I am gentle and lowly in heart, and you will find rest for your souls. For my yoke is easy, and my burden is light.

'ST JOHN'S AMBULANCE AT THE FOOTBALL MATCH'

It was during my times in emergency that I started to see that doctors and nurses were a big part of the healing process. As a healer, you can heal the body inside and help the body knit itself together faster, but I don't know how to put the plaster on the broken bones or stitch up a hand or finger back onto the body. Therefore, God and medical and science work well together.

One afternoon in emergency, a young girl was brought in by the paramedics. She had been at the football match when her pulse went quite low and she would not wake up. I quickly prayed quietly for her and her eyes opened, and her skin colour went back to normal. Then the nurses came and took her to a room to be monitored.

(If your pulse rate drops too low, you may feel lightheaded, dizzy, faint or very fatigued).

(If a child has too much sugar or medicine or even an adult has too much medicine, a healer can drain out most of the medicine that's hurting the victim).

Matthew 10:8

Heal the sick, cleanse the lepers, raise the dead, cast out devils: freely ye have received, freely give.

'GOD'S BIGGEST HEALING
WHEN THE SPIRIT WORLD COMES INTO THE REAL WORLD TO HONOUR GOD'

A nurse called me over to look after two small girls in emergency while they attended a patient. I brought the two girls books and pictures to colour in to keep them distracted. Then their dad caught my attention when he became quite concerned about the situation with his other sick daughter. The dad came over and showed me his daughter was quite ill.

The children then went back with their dad and I saw why the dad was concerned and thats when one of Jesus's biggest healing in emergency happened.

His little girl, about six years old, was not just pure white and grey but her face was pure green.

I have never seen a child look that ill and have a spirit sickness on her also. The doctor was very stressed as the girl looked too fatigued and her body had no colour.

(It was spiritual and a natural sickness.) I stayed with the parents and their daughter praying in the spirit until the green went and talked to the parents, letting them know that she was going to be alright but was very sick.

I knew I had to say 'God Bless' aloud to honour God's healing. The mother said the daughter had been run down for months since Christmas and the doctor and nurses were very concerned and allowed the blessing.

Genesis 2:7

And the Lord God formed a man from the dust of the ground, and breathed into his nostrils the breath of life, and the man became a living soul.

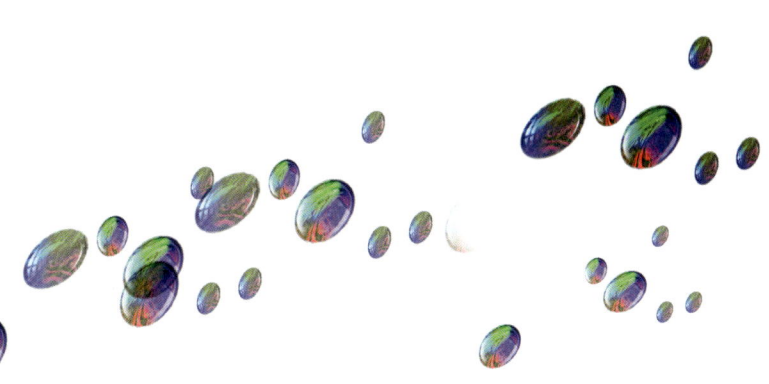

'DISABLED BOY: A HERO'

The secretaries in emergency were looking very sad. There were many sick children and a lot of smoke in the emergency from the fires surrounding the city. The smoke was caused by the burn offs to keep the shrubs from catching fire in the summer. But God was amazing; the smoke that was coming into the hospital disappeared and I knew it was God.

As I was preparing myself and was putting on my apron, I noticed a box of lollies left for the volunteers. I felt it was better to share them with the nurses, doctors and secretaries, as they deserved a treat. (A few lollies never hurt but too many can damage the body). I blessed the sweets so they would be like a medicine for everyone that had one.

The nurses, doctors and secretaries need to be blessed more as they see terror every day when they work in the hospital. They are fighting for children's lives and God knows that they all deserve a medal.

Later in the morning, a 14-year-old disabled boy, who couldn't talk and could hardly move and had a chest infection, was brought in. He was so helpless; so, I prayed to God aloud with the mother's permission to heal him more and prayed that God would heal everyone in his family.

Again, I pleaded to God, "Please heal him, Jesus." He could hardly breathe. "NOT FAIR," I cried and then I told the mum that she was a hero and that her son was an even bigger hero.

Job 33:4
The Spirit of God has made me, And the breath of the
Almighty gives me life.

'EMERGENCY… GOD REMOVES JELLYBEANS'

Emergency was too busy with nurses and doctors running everywhere and the waiting rooms were full
of parents with children who were sick with the flu and could not breathe.

The nurses and doctors always first select the ones that are too sick, over any of the ones that came
before them.

(This can upset the parents and it is often carefully explained why the nurses do this. If a child cannot
breathe or is in too much pain then they are to be brought in first.) Later, a little girl in emergency was
brought in by St John's Ambulance and the paramedics were very stressed as she could not breathe well
and had an oxygen mask on her mouth and it just wasn't working.

I went over to the little girl and with the parents' permission I started to pray and then I felt God start
to talk through me and his power entered her lungs. The little girl was healed as God's presence became
stronger so she could breathe easily again and then the oxygen mask could be removed.

Sugar can cause breathing difficulties, too many sweets (jellybeans) can make a child very ill. (It also
makes them jumpy and swirly).

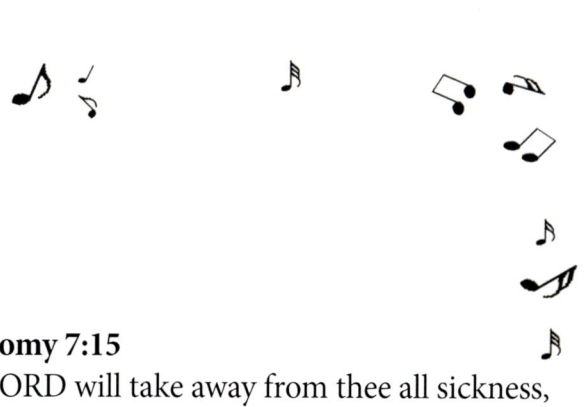

Deuteronomy 7:15
And the LORD will take away from thee all sickness,
and will put none of the evil diseases of Egypt, which
thou knowest, upon thee;
but will lay them upon all them that hate thee.

'JESUS CARRIES OUR BURDENS'

In emergency, I approached a dad and his son who was just flown in from up North of Australia by
The Flying Doctors.

He lay still on the bed as his dad cried beside him, sobbing. "I prayed at every stop that he would
live," said the dad.

The aboriginal dad was a Christian; then I saw the doctor staring at the boy heartbroken too and was
also crying.

I also was quite upset and went away quickly to cry quietly in another room because I knew it was a
bad accident. When I came back, I knew God wanted me to start to pray over the boy.

I knew God was healing the boy's brain and God started to give me words from the Holy Spirit to let
the dad know the boy was going to be okay and that many prayers from his people were coming in
also to heal his son.

Proverbs 4:20–22

My son pay attention to what I say; turn your ear to my words. Do not let them out of your sight, keep them within your heart; for they are life to those who find them and health to one's whole body.

'BLOOD DISORDER'

As I walked into emergency, I saw a small girl with a ladybug rug and pillow looking all sad and pale.
I went over to the girl and to her parents to say hello. The parents looked drained and exhausted with worry for their little girl.
They told me that their daughter had a blood disorder and asked me to pray.
I prayed for total recovery for the child and her family. The girl was on a drip, a tube that goes into their veins using a needle.
(Then the fluids and medicine can be given to the child directly into her body by the vein.)
I often tell the children that they are getting their breakfast through the tube when they complain about being hungry.

Jeremiah 30:17

I will restore you to health and heal your wounds, said the Lord.

'HARDEST SPIRITUAL HEALING'

Emergency was busy when I arrived in the morning and many sick children were being monitored by the nurses and doctors.

A biker dad was sitting next to his disabled son who couldn't move and was struggling to breathe and was on oxygen.

The boy was young and God showed me that he could be healed more. I went over to say hello to them and the dad explained his son's condition to me but he didn't want prayer for him.

I prophesied that his son would ride on his bike with him one day when he was older and explained that if the anointing of God is there in a church, everyone starts to get healed and the same happens at the hospital.

God showed me clearly that the dad and his son got healed spiritually and their bodies started to heal also.

(I was sick for a whole week from healing the boy and his dad).

Psalm 139:13–14

For you created my in most being; you knit me together in my mother's womb. I praise you because I am fearfully and wonderfully made; your works are wonderful; I know that full well.

'PRAYERS FOR AN UNBORN CHILD'

I felt my wings growing and surrounding the hospital today, I watched as they opened wide to protect the children.

Then I realized they weren't my wings but Gabriel's; this was always a blessing because God was sending his best angel to fight a battle in the hospital.

I didn't know why but I realised Gabriel was protecting the children upstairs as well as downstairs because God is a fair God and gives us all a choice to be healed by him.

Then I met a beautiful pregnant catholic lady in emergency. I prayed for her and the baby that was inside of her.

I told the mother that pregnant women do not know how stunning they are and they need to be told this more often and I knew her unborn child would be well as I see them holding their babies in the future.

Mark 10:13–16

People were bringing little children to Jesus for him to place his hands on them, but the disciples rebuked them. When Jesus saw this, he was indignant. He said to them, "Let the little children come to me, and do not hinder them,

for the kingdom of God belongs to such as these. Truly I tell you, anyone who will not receive the kingdom of God like a little child will never enter it." And he took the children in his arms, placed his hands on them and blessed them.

'BOY WITH HEART PROBLEMS'

When I arrived at the hospital in Emergency, a nurse asked me to make some coffee for parents in the observation room 4B.

As I went into the room, I saw a small boy with his mum who had stayed overnight. I asked the mother would she like a tea or coffee and then the boy started chatting, telling me he wanted to go home.

I heard God saying to my spirit that both the mother and son were unwell, and that God was wanting to repair them more.

The mother explained that the boy had a sore stomach and often came into the hospital for other conditions.

As an artist, if I draw, I can see what's in the person that is not well. So, I drew a picture on a paper towel to see what was wrong with him (it was his heart).

Isaiah 1:6

From the sole of the foot even unto the head there is no soundness in it; but wounds, and bruises, and putrifying sores: they have not been closed, neither bound up, neither mollified with ointment.

'SCHOOL SORES'

The afternoon in emergency was quiet and I was busy reading to a small boy when a mum and dad came in with their daughter quite stressed.

I later went over to ask if they wanted refreshments and just to have a chat with them. The mother and dad then asked me to pray for her. I prayed for total healing for the baby girl who had impetigo (school sores).

I let the parents know that my little boy too had school sores when younger. And every time they would heal, another sore appeared when a mosquito bit him. And he would scratch and in came another sore again, but with a lot of God and a little bit of medicine, it disappeared.

James 1:17
Every good gift and every perfect gift is from above, coming down from the Father of lights with whom there is no variation or shadow due to change.

'GOD'S GIFTS'

"Look, Dad, birds," said the little girl pointing at the nurses and me in emergency. We weren't birds but our spiritual wings were showing because the day was hard and many sick and hurting children had been coming into emergency.

The small girl was not that ill, but the dad was concerned, I only prayed in the spirit and gave them a blessing.

(Birds and animals can cause children to become very ill. It's why they must be kept clean and their environment kept disinfected). And when we take our children to the beach, we must be aware they are only small and need to be protected from what's in the water.

God gives us presents to keep us happy and well an example of this is a new baby, a new school, a new car, a new job or a husband.

'RASHES'

"Gossip, gossip, gossip," mumbled a nurse, "no sick children here; they bring their children in when they are well," she moaned.

A doctor smiled at her and yelled out in a bubbly voice, "Hello my dear, all is well in emergency today, yes?"

The nurse smiled, this nurse and doctor were God's favourites in emergency. He knew they fought for children's lives and God was making them stronger to fight his battle.

In the afternoon, a baby came into emergency with a rash. It looked like a heat rash but the parents wanted prayer. I then prayed for the whole family for protection and a great future and then God spoke to my spirit that the baby was healed.

I later met a beautiful mother in emergency whose son was hurt from an accident on a quad bike. He was upset because his mother and dad had taken the bike from him forever. I told the boy and his mother that the gift God gives to mothers is that he makes them powerful prophets of their children and that is why they take away things from their children because they know those things may harm them more in the future.

Again, later in the afternoon, another baby with a rash came into emergency, I thought just a fever rash but the parents wanted to be assured that their baby would go home well and asked me to say a prayer of healing over the baby, I did this and blessed them also.

(Sometimes they get worried that it might be meningitis, meningitis can cause a child to become very ill.)

41

Psalm 127:3
Children are a gift from the Lord;
they are a reward from him.

'BRAIN INJURY'

Security was posted at the doors to emergency and the glass door was locked when I arrived.
The nurses opened the door for me and as I entered, I heard lots of crying and screaming.
A teenage girl was stressed and not coping and wanted to go home, only she had to wait for her parents to pick her up. So they closed the door to keep her from running away.
The nurses chattered with the teenager and I also talked to her and brought in breakfast to keep her happy. The parents arrived later in the morning and as the teenager was leaving, the paramedics arrived with another teenager; a boy with a dreadful concussion followed by his parents who arrived at the same time.
I heard them explain quickly that the boy also had brain damage from birth and was in great pain. I felt God's presence surround Emergency as the anointing of God fell on the boy and the Holy Spirit was saying that God was removing the old damaged brain and repairing it.
Later, the dad talked to me for a while, explaining that he was involved in the Catholic Church and both him and the mother wanted prayer for their son.
The dad wanted to talk about his son's condition. He also told me he was a Sikh but was brought up in a Catholic school.
Jesus heals with love.

Revelation 22:2

It flowed down the centre of the main street. On each side of the river grew a tree of life, bearing twelve crops of fruit, with a fresh crop each month. The leaves were used for medicine to heal the nations.

'THE CHILDREN TOOK DAD'S TABLETS'

I arrived in emergency early in the morning and all was quiet and not many sick. Then St John's Ambulance arrived and brought in a sick little girl about two years old who was with her mother. The girl looked very drowsy and the nurses and doctors quickly came to help them and started monitoring the toddler. The dad and son arrived a little later and when all had settled down, I went to make sure all was okay and to see if they wanted refreshments. The mother told me that their little girl had taken dad's tablets and they were very worried.

The parents asked me to pray and so I blessed the whole family because I felt the little boy was also sick and that he might have also taken the tablets.

Jesus said their brains got hurt and he was healing both.

If I am unsure of a healing, I pray and wait on God to tell me if they are well.

Matthew 21:15–16

But when the chief priests and the scribes saw the wonderful things that he did, and the children crying out in the temple, "Hosanna to the Son of David!" they were indignant and they said to him, "Do you hear what these are saying?" And Jesus said to them, "Yes; have you never read, 'Out of the mouth of infants and nursing babies you have prepared praise'?"

'RASH MENINGITIS?'

Tonight, I prayed for many at emergency because it was very busy. One prayer was for a small girl with a rash. The mother was concerned and came over to me and wanted prayer for her daughter just in case it was meningitis. Symptoms of meningitis is muscle pain, pale blotchy skin, spots or rash and headaches.

Later, a toddler was laying on the emergency bed looking very unwell and had been rushed in by Saint John's Ambulance. I felt her sickness when I came to see if she would like some books to read. The mother told me that her little girl might have drank car coolant from her dad's shed and had brought the coolant with her to show the doctors.

I nearly cried in disbelief and prayed quickly with the permission of her mother. The child started to look brighter and I felt the sickness start to leave. I was so upset for the little girl, but God showed me he had healed her.

2 Chronicles 9:23
And all the kings of the earth sought the presence of Solomon, to hear his wisdom, that God had put in his heart.

'PROTECTION'

There were many tiny babies in emergency today and I knew Jesus was blessing all of them. The Power of the Holy Spirit came rushing in as I prayed for a little sick baby and I saw the Angel Gabriel arrive as I prayed for protection and good health for all the family.

This baby, God said, was very ill and needed more protection in case another attack occurred in the spirit realm. The baby's beautiful name was called Solomon, a name that is popular in the last few years as there has been a few other babies called Solomon in emergency, but each baby is unique even if they have the same name.

(The name Solomon belongs to a wise King in the bible).

Matthew 5:9
Blessed are the peacemakers, for they shall be
called sons of God.

'BABY COULDN'T BREATHE'

Emergency was quiet and some of the nurses were busy studying on the computer in the observation
ward while they had time. Other nurses where catching up with what was happening in the hospital.
I was busy bringing drinks to the parents and toys and books to the children.
One of the nurses was very chirpy but complaining in a lovely way about there not being enough
sheets available in the night shift. This nurse's voice is always delightful, and she is like sunshine to
Emergency. I told her later she reminds me of my youngest daughter.
Later, a sad little baby boy was rushed into emergency by the ambulance. The baby could hardly
breathe. The nurses rushed in and quickly put the oxygen mask on the baby. Mum was sobbing and
the baby was crying too much. Later the mother asked for prayer and after prayer the little boy laid
peacefully without fighting the oxygen mask.
(Jesus sent help)
(God's anointing was powerful)
(God's peace is different to man's peace)

Luke 9:42 -

As the boy came forward, the demon knocked him to the ground and threw him into a violent convulsion. But Jesus rebuked the evil spirit and healed the boy. Then he gave him back to his father.

'SEIZURES'

The nurses were giggling about the Christmas decorations around the desk which was wrapped with old-fashioned brown paper and lots of decorations. In every area of emergency, Santa and reindeer balloons were floating on the ceiling and all the children looked quite delighted.

Many volunteers were handing out the balloons to make the sick children happy.

Later in the morning, I met a lovely mother who was stressed because her little boy was having seizures and they wouldn't stop. The mother asked me to pray because her son had many other illnesses. I prayed for a full recovery, the boy seemed strong and yet so sick.

Luke 9:58
And Jesus said to him, "The foxes have holes and the birds of the air have nests, but the Son of Man has nowhere to lay His head."

'BASKETBALL'

There were many unwell teenagers in emergency; a lot of them hurt badly from sports. I explained to parents that to be involved in sports is good and keeps teenagers away from crime. Only it would be nicer if they had sports uniforms that protected the body more like the American rugby uniforms. A boy, 13-or-14-year-old, came into emergency very upset with his arm broken; he looked grey and tired. I spoke to him and his parents and I commented on his football shoes but he laughed and said they are basketball shoes. The parents told me he had hurt himself at the basketball and the break was bad. The boy looked too sad and distraught so I prayed in the spirit quietly for the family.

Jeremiah 29:12
Then you will call upon me and come and pray to me, and I will hear you.

'HERNIA'

St John's Ambulance paramedics brought a girl into Emergency who had hernia in her groin. The girl's legs had gone weak underneath her and she had collapsed. The girl told the nurse her pain scale was 10. She allowed prayer with her mum present. God's anointing was for her that day.
(Hernia is when part of an organ or tissue in the body pushes through a weak spot in a muscle wall, it can then go into a space where it does not belong in the body.
This protrusion is a hernia, which may look like a lump).

Proverbs 25:27
It is not good to eat much honey, nor is it glory to search out one's own glory.

'FLICKED BY AN ANGEL'

A boy in Emergency looked so ill, his skin was grey and his veins looked green.
I wanted to make sure he was going to be okay. As I walked past, I saw an angel come
out of me and flick the boy well, the angel belonged to God and was Gabriel.
(Gabriel is a powerful angel who looks after children) I have seen Gabriel a few times. One amazing
time to show me clearly that he will be there to look after the telethon children and another time
after a loss of a child who I never got to meet and God sent Gabriel to wrap his wings around the
broken church that lost the boy.

Matthew 15:17
Do you not understand that everything that goes into the mouth passes into the stomach, and is eliminated.

'SMITH WIGGLESWORTH'

There is a story of a great prophet of God called Smith Wigglesworth who could heal the dying and one of his main healing was stopping appendicitis. He also said that Australia was the place that God would use to create revival worldwide. An Australian aboriginal prophet also said this would happen. His name was Guboo Ted Thomas.

Later in the morning a boy from Joondalup came into Emergency. His stomach was sore and he was sobbing. But then he stopped crying as they put him on the hospital bed.

He said the pain had gone. The parents told the nurse it was diagnosed as suspected appendicitis. I knew God healed the boy. I did not pray aloud, only in the spirit. (God healed him fast to bless him.) Appendicitis occurs when the appendix (extension) of the colon becomes inflamed and infected.

Isaiah 12:3
With joy you will draw water from the wells of salvation.

'THE ANGEL NURSE AND THE HAPPY BABY'

The main nurse in emergency was running around busy, attending many of the sick children. I admired this nurse; she is a strong older nurse who can be a little grumpy but always gentle and kind. God knows she cares a lot and as a prophet of God, I saw God giving her a trumpet for end times. (Prophets of God are much like a clairvoyant; they see the future that God reveals to them). The other nurses in Emergency were all huddled together having a chat about the children when I saw a favourite Emergency male nurse walk in. He had his spiritual wings on his back, and greeted them and said," I've been away for a while upstairs with all the other crazy nurses." As the male nurse started attending to each sick child, he became the hunchback of Notre dame and in the spirit, he had the hump on his back. (God loves comedy and fun, he created us in his own image).
Later, I met a beautiful mum and her baby in Emergency, the baby was 5-months-old and had a colossal bag attached to him, but had always been a happy baby with lots of energy. The parents asked me to pray for them and their child and after prayer I explained to mum the process of it not being me but the outflow of the Holy Spirit that heals powerfully. The mum was fit but sad. I prayed again later for protection for her and angels would be close every time she was being hurt.

BOY BLIND
A baby seven month old
with his mother and his grandmother
came into emergency because they
were worried about his condition.
The boy was blind and not well
they allowed me to pray, my prayers
were simple but came from God.
I was feeling sad for all the sick
children and had asked
God who the annoiting was for this
day in emergency and he said
this little baby boy.
The babies problem I didn't
understand but he comes in
every month I know
God worked a miracle.

John 9

Jesus Heals a Man Born Blind

As he went along, he saw a man blind from birth. His disciples asked him, "Rabbi, who sinned, this man or his parents, that he was born blind?"

"Neither this man nor his parents sinned," said Jesus, "but this happened so that the works of God might be displayed in him. As long as it is day, we must do the works of him who sent me. Night is coming, when no one can work. While I am in the world, I am the light of the world."

After saying this, he spit on the ground, made some mud with the saliva, and put it on the man's eyes. "Go," he told him, "wash in the Pool of Siloam" (this word means "Sent"). So the man went and washed, and came home seeing.

'BOY BLIND'

In Emergency, it had been a very sad and a dreadful week and many children were hurt. I felt upset for all in the hospital. Then God showed me that Emergency staff had fought great battles and he wanted to reward them and that things were going to change soon and He was getting them ready for many miracles.

Later in the day, a seven-month-old baby with his mother and his grandmother came into Emergency; they were worried about his condition. The boy was blind and not well. They allowed me to pray, my prayers were simple but came from God. (I know God worked a miracle).

Isaiah 54:13

All your children shall be taught by the LORD, and great shall be the peace of your children.

'PEACE IN EMERGENCY'

I read to the sick children this night, instead of praying in Emergency (it's praying in a unique way). It was peaceful in emergency and the nurses and doctors were having coffees and catching up with the latest news of the hospital. The secretaries were chatting and the parents and children seemed calm. I knew it was God's presence that was helping everyone tonight. The doctors and nurses had a hard week and were recharging but still on high alert, for anything can happen when in Emergency.

Psalm 34:18

The Lord is near to the broken- hearted and saves the crushed in spirit.

'A BEAUTIFUL ABORIGINAL BOY'

Gods anointing today was for a two-month-old aboriginal baby. I did not pray aloud, only in the spirit. I blessed the baby's head and the middle of his forehead between his eyebrows to close the spirit eye.

This stops bad spirits attacking the baby. I knew the Holy Spirit was healing his heart and lungs. (Jesus heals powerfully.)

Exodus 23:25

And you shall serve the LORD your God, and he shall bless your bread, and your water; and I will take sickness away from the middle of you.

'WHOPPING COUGH BABY'

A baby with whopping cough came to Emergency from a country town. The mother said the baby had coughed all night, so they caught the train to the hospital to get more help.
I prayed straight away when I knew it was whopping cough and I told her that God does not fail. I knew the baby had suffered too much and her eye was sore from coughing.
I had to wait a whole hour before God said the baby was okay and then I knew I could say that they were very lucky that God created a miracle… Amen.

Matthew 6:17
But thou, when thou fastest, anoint thine head, and wash thy face.

'MUSLIM BOY HAVING SEIZURES'

Paramedics brought a boy into the hospital's Emergency early in the morning as I was arriving. I went over to the paramedics and the boy. The parents quickly told me he had fitted once before, then had another seizure and there was no reason why. I helped the parents settle down as the nurses and doctors checked the child's pulse.

They wanted me to pray for their son even though they were Muslims. After prayer, the boy got up and felt better. I knew that he was well. God does it in a cool way.

Exodus 23:25

Worship the LORD your God, and His blessing will be on your food and water. I will take away sickness from among you.

'DYSTONIA SPASMS'

A baby boy who was only five months old was very sad with a sore throat. The nurse said the baby had dystonia spasms in his throat. I prayed only in the spirit as I was in another part of the hospital. Then I just held the baby so Jesus could heal him.

Dystonia is uncontrollable muscle spasms caused by wrong signals from the brain. Dystonia may get better or worse or stay the same, but with Jesus' blessing, the children can be healed more.

Great Healers of God can completely heal the brain if the child does not have too much medicine.

Like all things, a balanced life of anything keeps us healthy and strong.

Jeremiah 1:5

Before I formed thee in the belly I knew thee; and
before thou camest forth out of the womb I sanctified
thee, [and]
I ordained thee a prophet unto the nations.

'BROKEN ARM'

On a Saturday in the hospital Emergency, it is always busy with sports accidents which is scary for the
children and parents. The nurses and doctors also become very stressed as too many children get injured.
I prayed for many with concussion or sore necks because this area is what keeps their bodies active.
(The brain is important and needs more protection when playing contact sports). Today, a rugby
player with a broken arm came into the hospital and was with his Mother, they were from New
Zealand. I prayed for the boy because he looked very unwell. I am always sad when I see them with
arms broken and I let them know that it happened to my son at school.
I always tell them that when I was a teenager, I wanted a broken arm. I thought it would be nice to
have a signed plaster. I know a lot of children think this but in reality, it's just painful.
When I pray, I ask God to show me what he is healing most. Sometimes it's not just the broken arm,
it could be something in their brain or their heart.

Jeremiah 29:11
'For I know the plans I have for you,' declares the
LORD, 'plans to prosper you and not to harm you,
plans to give you hope and a future.'

'RUGBY'

A young boy was hurt at rugby and a rugby mother called for St John's Ambulance to help him and
he was then transported to the hospital to Emergency.

Later, a boy from the same game at rugby arrived in the St John's Ambulance to Emergency.

The mother of the boy explained that she called for the ambulance for another boy then her son got
hurt and ended up in emergency too.

I prayed for both boys and for their brains; the mothers wanted prayers for them. I also prophesied
about their future wellness.

Luke 9:11
But the crowds learned about it and followed him. He welcomed them and spoke to them about the kingdom of God, and healed those who needed healing.

'TWINS'

A dad in emergency, with his baby, was looking very concerned and the doctor was talking to him for a long time. The nurses then came in to set up an infusion needle in the baby's hand just in case the baby needed extra fluids.
I went to see the dad to have a chat and offer him a tea or coffee; the dad was still looking worried. He said he had twin babies and told me one of the babies was in intensive care upstairs in the hospital.
The dad then asked me to pray for them. After I prayed for the babies, I knew God was healing them.

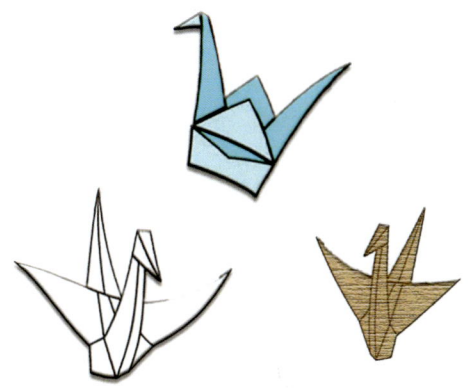

Matthew 19:14 "Let the children come to me, and do not prevent them;
for the Kingdom of Heaven belongs to such as these."

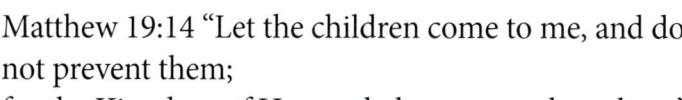

'A PRAYER FOR A MUSLIM BABY'

I love the finger puppets that the volunteer ladies make in Emergency especially when the colours are the football colours. The children love to choose the colours of their favourite football team. The day was quiet and not many children were sick. I didn't say that it's quiet out loud because nurses' superstition is that they believe that it will become busy later. (I don't believe in superstitions but I honour their belief). In the afternoon, a baby, 4 weeks old, was brought into the hospital who was very ill and the parents were concerned. The parents were Muslims but let me pray a blessing on the whole family and a healing in Jesus' name on the baby.
When it comes to saving a child's life, a blessing from a powerful God is the strongest medicine.

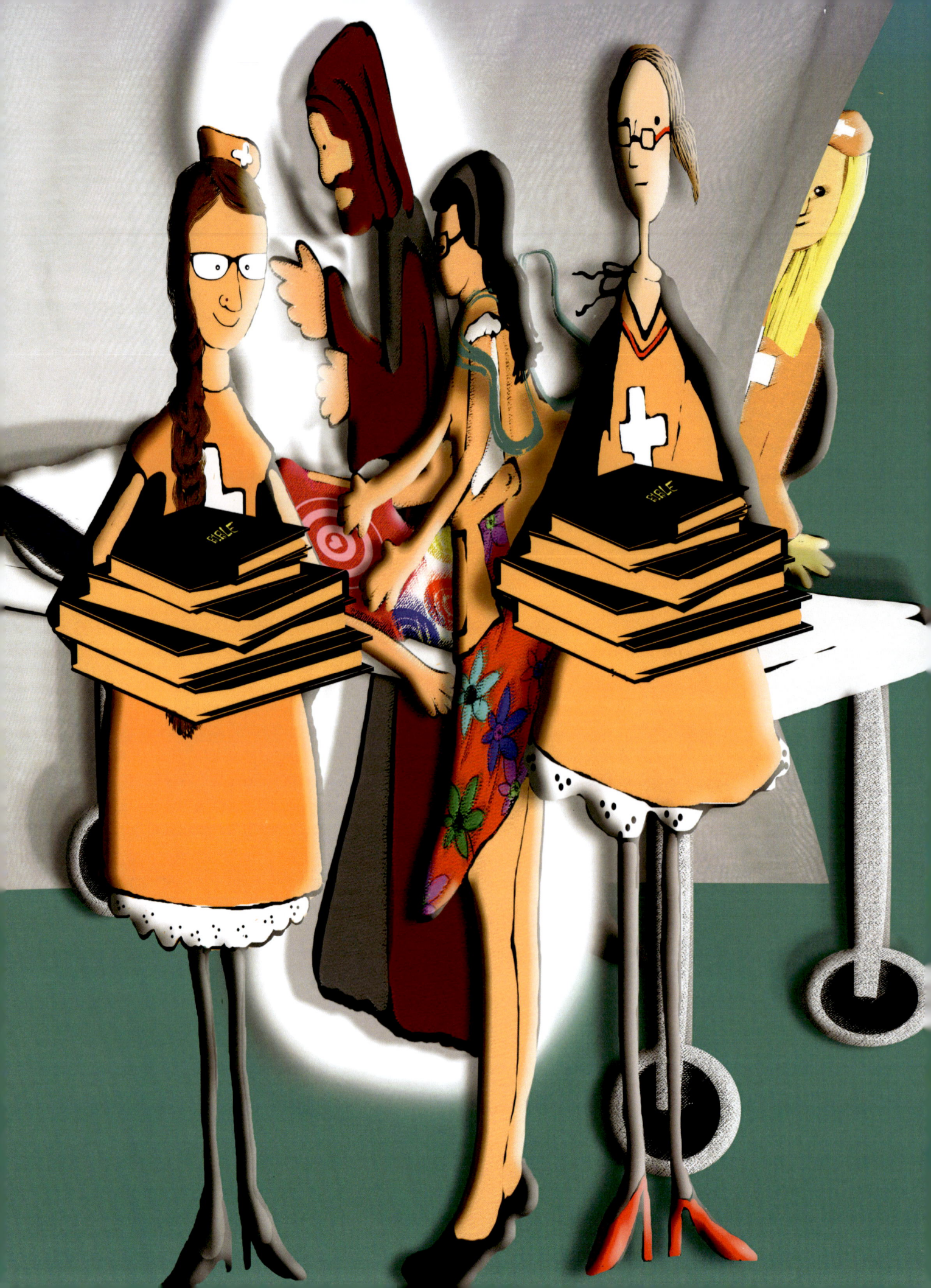

Matthew 19:2
Large crowds followed him, and he healed them there.

'DIABETES 1'

A young girl, 15, with diabetes 1 was blessed by Jesus in Emergency.
(Her mother agreed for prayer). As a strong healer I know that God can heal diabetes 1 but eating
right and listening to the body and listening to God and the doctor's advice is also important.
As our bodies start to heal, God will show us what he is healing in us each day and as we believe in
God's healing, one day the illness will no longer be there.
To fight a sentence of sickness by going for your dreams and not letting the sickness stop you and as
time passes, the healing will happen.
God is hope.

Exodus 23:25

And you shall serve the LORD your God, and he shall
bless your bread, and your water; and
I will take sickness away from the middle of you.

'PRAYED FOR AN ATHEIST'S SON'

I felt God's presence was very strong in the hospital as I prayed for so many in the Emergency.
Later in the morning, I met a Russian dad who had been in Australia for 30 years and his son was
very ill with a heart condition.
The boy wanted prayer and the Dad agreed but said he was an atheist.
(I thanked God as I prayed that I would meet an atheist in Emergency and that he would see Jesus.
And God answered that prayer).

Psalm 91: 9–10
"Because thou hast made the LORD, which is my refuge, even the most High, thy habitation; There shall no evil befall thee, neither shall any plague come nigh thy dwelling."

'PRAYED FOR MANY TODAY'

As I walked into the hospital, the waiting room was filled with old tissues everywhere and pencils scattered, and sick hats left on the floor and messy fingerprints from the many sick children that had visited Emergency overnight.

I felt sad for the doctors and nurses. They had a busy night and looked weary. The Holy Spirit took over and I started to pray for the many sick children.

Later, a worried young boy about seven years old couldn't be diagnosed so his dad let me pray and the boy left well.

Our God is a wonderful God.

Proverbs 4:20–25

God says, "Give attention to my words; Incline your ear to my sayings. Do not let them depart from your eyes; Keep them in the midst of your heart; For they are life to those who find them, And health to all their flesh."

'FOSTER DAD'

I talked to a foster Dad from up North, whose son was a two-year-old aboriginal boy. The boy had been sick with a lot of different illnesses and the foster dad was concerned. God blessed the dad with a prophecy and then I prayed for the boy's healing.

Another little aboriginal boy came into Emergency, quite well and happy with too much energy, jumping here and there. Only the little boy had a dog bite on his mouth; it was a terrible bite and he was flown in by The Flying Doctors from another town up North.

All the nurses, doctors and myself spoilt him rotten, he was such a delight.

Mathew 18:19–20
"Again I say to you that if two of you agree on Earth concerning anything that they ask, it will be done for them by My Father in heaven. For where two or three are gathered together in My name, I am there in the midst of them."

'I WANT TO GO HOME'

Before entering the hospital, I stopped and prayed for a little boy who wanted to go home.
He had a drip in his arm and the dad said he had a blood or bone disease, and they were getting fresh air.
I knew Jesus was right there. I asked them if they wanted prayer; dad and son agreed… when two or more agree in Jesus' name then the prayer is answered.

Ecclesiastes 10:17
Blessed [art] thou, O land, when thy king [is] the son of nobles, and thy princes eat in due sea- son, for strength, and not for drunkenness!

'EATING DISORDER'

A teenager was struggling with an eating disorder and wanted prayer. The mother agreed and I explained about another girl who had an eating disorder but now was healthy and becoming a nurse. I prayed for her to become well and that she would do great things.
(Isn't Jesus funny the way he heals outside of the box, praying in Emergency where the real sick need help).

Matthew 8:16

"When the even was come, they brought unto him many that were possessed with devils: and he cast out the spirits with his word, and healed all that were sick:"

'MULTIPLE SCLEROSIS'

In Emergency, a boy about 13 or 14 years old had a sore leg and foot and had a mild form of multiple sclerosis.

I prayed that Jesus would totally heal him and remove his diseases.

The mother agreed in prayer and again when two agreed that God answers prayer, God heals powerfully and by trusting God we can keep moving forward.

God heals brains if He can cure brain damage from a car accident then why can He not cure other brain injuries? The body then must practice moving again like a baby learning to crawl, then parts of our body that have been affected by the disease need to become strong again.

God can heal us but we must get up and walk again.

Corinthians 12:12–14

One Body but Many Parts

12 There is one body, but it has many parts. But all its many parts make up one body. It is the same with Christ. 13 We were all baptized by one Holy Spirit. And so we are formed into one body. It didn't matter whether we were Jews or Gentiles, slaves or free people. We were all given the same Spirit to drink. 14 So the body is not made up of just one part. It has many parts.

'KIDNEY DYSPLASIA'

The nurses in Emergency were very busy and were worried about a small boy.

I went to see the boy to offer toys and books, only he was very tired.

The parents said their son had kidney dysplasia and they wanted a prayer for him. I prayed for total healing in Jesus' mighty name.

Kidney dysplasia is when the kidney does not form correctly in the womb.

(The mother was a Catholic and dad was an Anglican).

'Where there is faith, God works his miracles.'

to dear jesus your time and my time is the best time I am writing this now to say that your my valentine jesus and thank you for the beautiful gift you have given me...

2 John 1:3

Grace be with you, mercy, [and] peace, from God the Father, and from the Lord Jesus Christ, the Son of the Father, in truth and love.

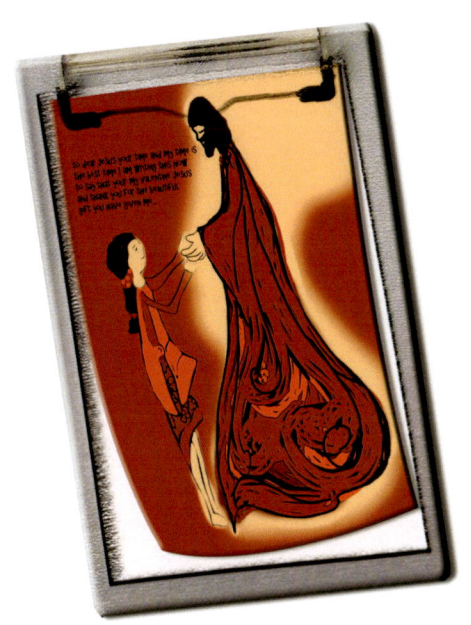

'BABY WITH WINGS'

In emergency, I saw a baby with wings on her back in the spirit. The mother asked if I would pray for her baby. I prayed for the baby girl even though I felt she wasn't sick.

(When I see wings on a baby, it means something might happen to them later in the future.)

Then God showed me the baby running around happily in the future.

"Funny how cots look like little jail cells."

'The cots were not around until the 19th century and children used to sleep in their mother's bed and parents would sleep in different rooms.'

John 17:3
And this is life eternal, that they might know thee the
only true God, and Jesus Christ, whom thou hast sent.

'LIVER TRANSPLANT'

At the hospital, I was busy collecting the newspapers for Emergency when I saw a dad wheeling his
little girl in her stroller.

I stopped to say hello and the dad spoke to me saying that his daughter was unwell and asked me to
pray for her.

I prayed for his daughter that she would completely recover then went back to Emergency.

The dad later came up to me and told me his daughter had had a liver transplant at 7 months and
now was 2 years old.

I felt sad for the dad and his daughter, and explained that my friend's daughter had a liver transplant
at 3 years but was now an adult becoming a nurse. The dad left happy as God is the God of hope.

Isaiah 53:5

But he [was] wounded for our transgressions, [he was] bruised for our iniquities: the chastisement of our peace [was] upon him; and with his stripes we are healed.

'IRISH BABY'

God's anointing in emergency was for a new-born baby who was only 5 weeks old. The baby had breathing problems and her mother was Irish and very stressed.

I was so sad and scared that the baby girl was struggling to breathe. The mother was very frightened and talked for a while and told me the baby's unique name. It had to do with horses.

I told the mother that babies are the toughest bosses in the world they don't let you sit down, and they keep you up all night. And these little bosses have a stressful life because they were all snug in their world in the womb and then they come out to a whole new world (their new job). So, they need a dummy sometimes just to help them when things get too tough.

1 Corinthians 1:9
God [is] faithful, by whom ye were called unto the fellowship of his Son Jesus Christ our Lord.

'STRONG TWINS'

As I entered Emergency, I looked and saw that every hospital bed was full, and it was only early morning. The nurses looked too busy, so I quickly went and helped and offered toys, books or drinks to the families.

I met a lovely couple who were nursing two strong twin babies. Both babies lay on the bed; one was crying, the other baby lay peacefully. The peaceful baby was the sickest. I felt the heaviness of the flu on the baby.

The twins had influenza; the parents explained, and they were very worried for the youngest twin because he was so lifeless. Then both babies started to look better after a while and the parents asked me to pray to protect the children more.

I knew the anointing of Jesus was for these twins so I prayed a blessing and a prophecy over their lives that they would grow stronger and stay well.

2 John 1:3

Grace be with you, mercy, [and] peace, from God the Father, and from the Lord Jesus Christ, the Son of the Father, in truth and love.

'TUMOUR IN THE KNEE'

"Could someone go and see the family in number 14?" said a nurse in Emergency, "they might need a coffee they as have been told sad news that the daughter has a tumour." I went quickly as I knew it could not be cancer as God promises He removes cancer through His anointing.

A small family surrounded a girl on the hospital bed, the young girl had a scar on her knee. I asked the family if they would like a refreshment, but the mother only wanted to talk about her daughter. The Holy Spirit started to speak through me as I let the girl know that she reminded me of my own daughter and how beautiful and loving she is.

And when my own daughter had sicknesses, God always pulled her through and sent help. The mother told me the daughter had a tumour. Then God spoke to me and said she was well.

The mother then asked for prayer so that her daughter would be completely healed. I prayed a blessing on the family and that no more sad things would happen to her daughters.

Genesis 18:4
"Please let a little water be brought and wash your feet,
and rest yourselves under the tree.

'GLASS IN FOOT'

A little girl in emergency was dressed up in the prettiest lacy dress I had ever seen. It
reminded me of the 1980s fashion for little girls.
Her dad was overly concerned which melted my heart as his little girl had glass deeply embedded in
her foot and she needed surgery.
I understood his concern because the little girl would have to have a general anaesthesia to put her
to sleep before surgery and sometimes complications can arise.
The dad then asked me if I would pray to make sure all would go well so I prayed for the little girl
that Jesus would keep her safe.

Matthew 6:10
Thy kingdom come. Thy will be done in earth,
as [it is] in heaven.

'GIRL UNWELL'

An overly thin sickly girl was brought into the Emergency. She was very weak and unwell. As the girl
lay on her hospital bed, she was too weak to move when her mother asked her to say hello to me.
I let her daughter know we had some magazines for both of them for when she felt better while they
waited for the doctor to see them. The little girl smiled and started to look well and got up slightly
and I raised the bed so she could sit up more.
The mother was surprised that her girl was feeling better and then asked me if I would pray for her.
The daughter agreed for prayer and I prayed for healing for her mum because her mother looked
very unwell too and also was very thin.
Jesus blesses and helps always.

Psalms: 37–24

Though he fall, he shall not be utterly cast down: for the Lord upholdeth him with his hand.

'GIRL FELL OFF HER SCOOTER'

A 15-year-old girl who fell off her scooter was brought into Emergency by St John's Ambulance.
I went to visit the girl to see if she needed anything while she waited for her parents to arrive.
She chattered to me and I knew she was very unwell and worried, so I stayed for a while until the doctor and nurses came back. I prayed for her in the spirit until her parents came.
God spoke to me that he healed the girl's brain and that she was going to be okay.

Revelation 21:4

"He will wipe every tear from their eyes. There will be no more death or mourning or crying or pain, for the old order of things has passed away."

'BOY'S FACE BURNT'

A boy in emergency was badly burnt and was crying and finding it hard to breathe.

His face was blistered and raw and he was very upset. His mum told me that his face was burnt by hot soup.

I talked to him about what he likes to do at school or what sports he plays, to take his mind off his injury. He started talking a little and I noticed he was breathing well again.

Then I felt the power of God wash over Emergency. (Jesus helps us when we pray to him and the Holy Spirit in us can renew our minds). God does not like that children cannot breathe and sends help. With God and medical science working together, many can be healed.

Exodus 23:25

25 Worship the LORD your God, and his blessing will be on your food and water. I will take away sickness from among you.

'BABY BURNT WITH HOT WATER'

A distressed mother and dad came running into emergency, crying with their baby
boy in their arms. The baby boy was burnt with hot water.
The blisters were bad, and the baby was sobbing in between screams.
The nurses quickly took the baby to wash him with cool water which upset the baby even more. The sobbing was too sad and the other children close by started to cry.
I helped the nurse as she talked to the doctor and let the water cool the burns. And I prayed in the spirit that the baby would be totally healed and to take away the pain.
The baby then fell asleep; I know Jesus calmed the baby.

Psalms 30:2

O LORD my God, I cried out to You, And You
healed me.

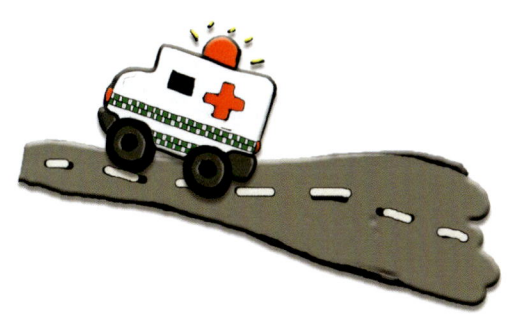

'BOY WITH BRONCHITIS'

The emergency was full of coughing and sniffing as winter had arrived and with it many sick
children. One toddler was bored but very ill so I carried him around for a little while to give the
parents a rest.

The boy was so heavy with pneumonia; I had never felt a sickness this heavy in a child before. My
arms ached carrying him and I felt the sickness leaving as I continually prayed in the spirit and then
gave him back to the dad.

Then another little baby had bronchitis and was very ill, which is always a concern especially if the
baby is too small.

I prayed for the baby with bronchitis at the request of the parents and also prayed a blessing on
the whole family.

Exodus 23:25

So you shall serve the LORD your God, and He will bless your bread and your water. And I will take sickness away from the midst of you.

'BRAIN HAEMORRHAGE'

Later in the morning in Emergency, the paramedics arrived with a distraught boy who had been hurt badly at a football game. The mother came and told me what was wrong with her son that the doctors where checking for brain haemorrhages and she was very worried.
(Brain haemorrhage is 'bleeding in the brain). I brought them lots of toast and drinks while they waited for the boy to get better. I prophesied that her son would be well and have a healthy brain. (Prophesied means to tell the future from God).

Luke 21:26

Men's hearts failing them from fear and the expectation
of those things which are coming on the earth, for the
powers of the heavens will be shaken.

'BOY'S HEART RACING'

Two nurses in the hospital's emergency were fixing a boy's leg that was broken.
The boy was screaming in fear that his leg was going to hurt more. The nurses where trying to calm
the boy but he was getting too upset, eventually the plaster was applied.
The mother told me that the boy's leg was broken for the second time, that's why he was scared. The
boy's heart was racing too fast; sometimes our hearts fail us because of fear.
God spoke that it was the boy's heart that he was healing.

Luke 18:27

But He said, "The things which are impossible with men are possible with God."

'BABY WITH A CYST'

A delightful grandmother, mother and toddler came into the emergency.

I introduced myself asking if they would like a toy for their child.

They busily started chatting about their beautiful boy and his condition.

The little boy had a large cyst on his mouth the size of a tennis ball and they asked me
if I would pray for him.

I agreed and prayed aloud to God, asking Him to powerfully remove whatever was causing the cyst
in Jesus' mighty name.

Matthew 14:36

And besought him that they might only touch the hem of his garment: and as many as touched were made perfectly whole.

'BABY NOT A GOOD COLOUR'

It was a busy morning in the Emergency and many children with sore necks and concussions from rugby and football were resting on the hospital beds. The Emergency was also filled with many children vomiting from the flu virus, so things were looking messy and many of the nurses were running around too busy to stop and rest.

I was busy helping the nurses make beds and tidying the waiting room and talking to the parents and children when Saint John's Ambulance arrived and brought in a very ill baby boy and his dad into emergency.

The baby was not a good colour and the doctor was concerned. The dad explained that the baby could not keep the fluids down. They were scared for the baby's health.

I prayed later that the baby and the family would be well and that the baby would grow up strong like the dad.

Before I left the hospital, I asked God if he would fully heal everyone in the Emergency and hospital of something that they would never be cured of and I thank Jesus every day for blessing that prayer with a 'yes'.

THE CHARACTERS PLAYING AN INSTRUMENT REPRESENTS 1, 2 AND 3 NURSES IN EMERGENCY AND MYSELF. THE NURSE BLOWING THE TRUMPET REPRESENTS AN OLDER NURSE WHO IS A TRUMPET BLOWER FOR GOD.
THE NURSE PLAYING THE GUITAR IS ONE SHORT NURSE WHO IS A SAMSON. THE NURSE PLAYING THE DRUMS REPRESENT AN OLDER SHORT NURSE AND AN OLDER SECRETARY AND THEY WILL BE LEADERS FOR GOD.
AND THE LADY PLAYING THE BOX GUITAR IS THE POKADOT BOW NURSE WITH DARK HAIR AND MYSELF WHO ARE LEADERS FOR GOD.
THE BLONDE NURSE REPRESENTS FOUR NURSES
TWO SHORT BLONDE NURSES AND ONE TALL BLONDE NURSE AND ONE STRONG NURSE. THEY CARRY THE BASKET OF SUMMER FRUITS THAT WILL WARN GOD'S PEOPLE.

King James Bible
And he said, Amos, what seest thou? And I said, A basket of summer fruit.
Then said the LORD unto me,
The end is come upon my people of Israel; I will not again pass by them anymore.

(THE BLACK AND WHITE NURSE CARTOON IS A PROPHETIC IMAGE DESIGNED A YEAR OR MORE BEFORE I WENT TO EMERGENCY).

The bible verses where taken from different bible versions that were

HOLY SPIRIT LEAD

The New International Version (NIV)
is a completely original translation of the Bible developed by more than one hundred scholars working from the best available Hebrew, Aramaic, and Greek texts.

The Living Bible (TLB or LB) translation by Kenneth Taylor Modern language bible and it is to very easy to read and understand. Also a Catholic version.

King James Version (KJV)
Difficult to read and understand due to 17th Century vocabulary and style.
New King James Version (NKJV)
1982. Taken directly from KJV but with more modern words. Choppy reading because it maintains 17th Century sentence structure. New Living Translation (NLT)
Highly readable in vocabulary and language. Does not use original or recently discovered sources.
English Standard Version (ESV)
2001. A literal translation that makes use of recently discovered sources. Easier reading than other word for word translations

THE CHARACTERS OF THIS BOOK
ARE THE DOCTORS AND
NURSES, SECRETARIES, PCA'S
AND
CLEANERS IN EMERGENCY AND
ALL HAVE AN ELISHA
ANNOITING ON THEM..

Never give up.

A BOOK OF REAL MIRACLES

in Western Australia
a doctor prayed for help to save the children and
GOD DECIDED TO MAKE A HOSPITAL AN OPEN HEAVEN